GW00417373

WE RECOMMEND PUTTING A BLANK SHEET O
PAPER BEHIND YOUR ARTWORK WHEN USING
MARKERS TO PREVENT BLEED THROUGH.

GUDRUN HALL
WWW.THEBLUEOFMYEYE.COM

COLOR TEST SHEET

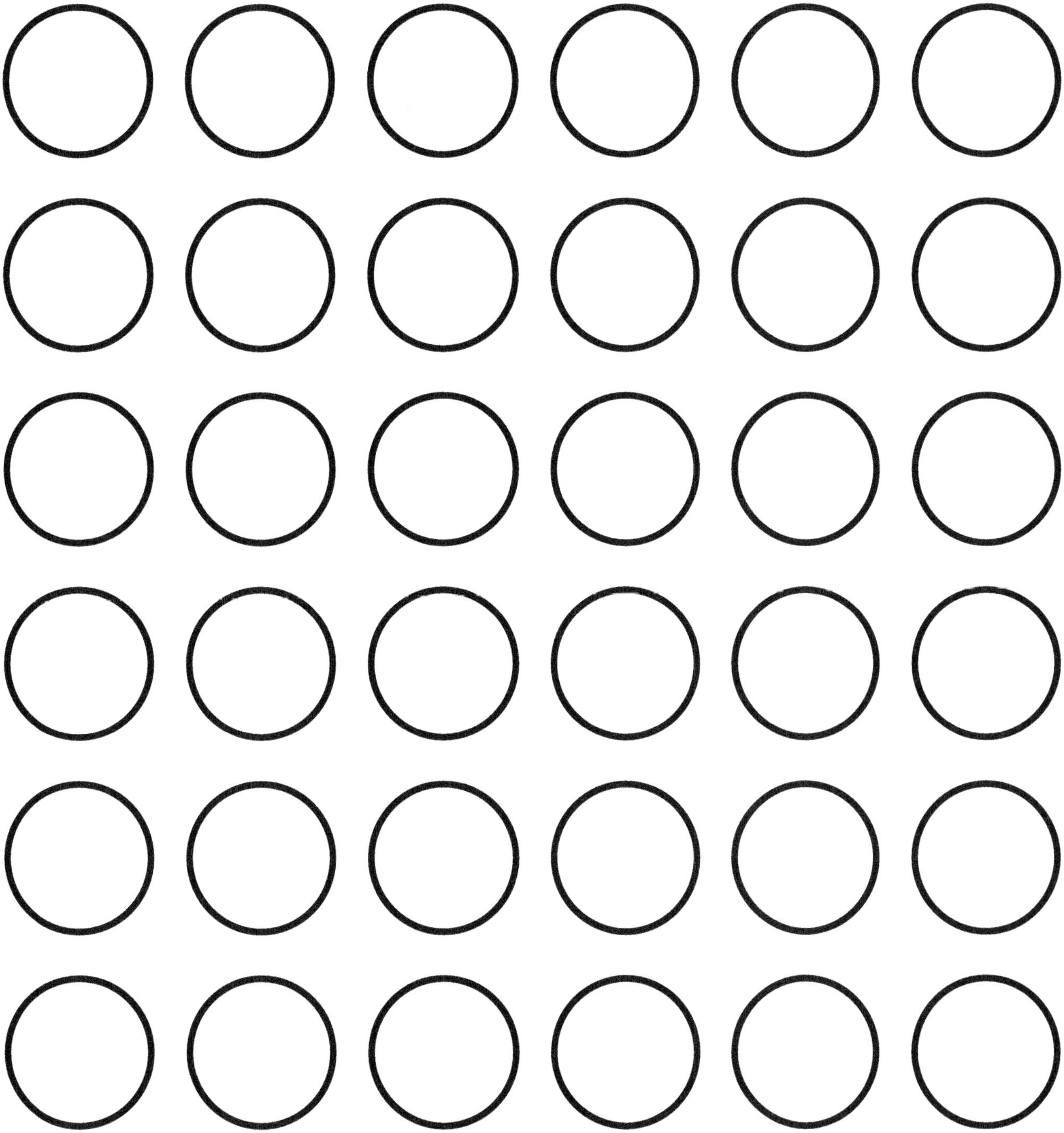

COLOR TEST SHEET

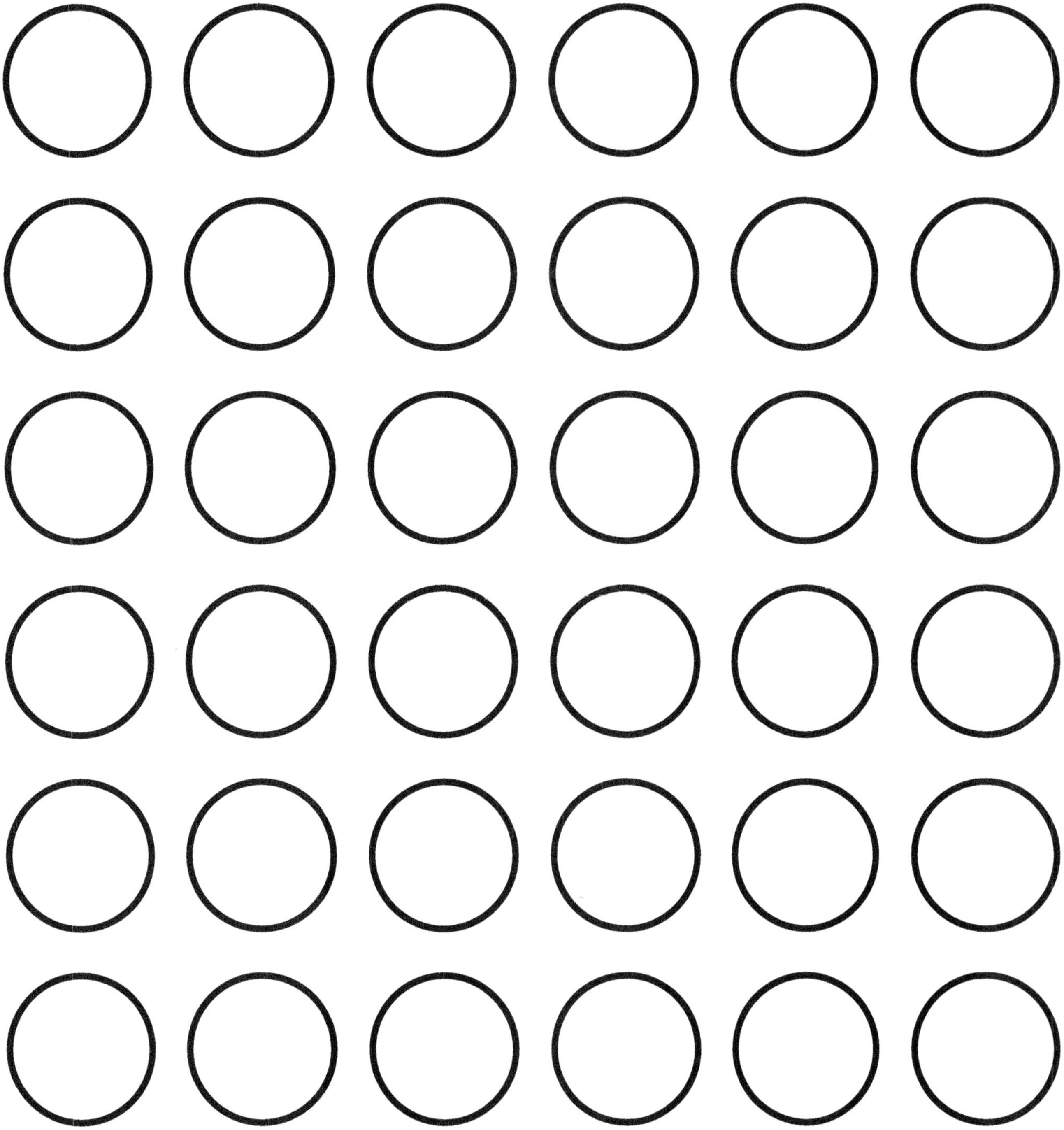

Printed in Great Britain
by Amazon

22690273R00051